ADAM HAMILTON

Enough

REVISED EDITION

Discovering Joy Through Simplicity and Generosity

Leader Guide

by Sally D. Sharpe

Abingdon Press / Nashville

ENOUGH
DISCOVERING JOY THROUGH
SIMPLICITY AND GENEROSITY
REVISED EDITION
LEADER GUIDE

ISBN 978-1-5018-5790-4

18 19 20 21 22 23 24 25 26 27 — 10 9 8 7 6 5 4 3 2 1
MANUFACTURED IN THE UNITED STATES OF AMERICA

CONTENTS

How to Use This Leader Guide 5

Week One
When Dreams Become Nightmares 9

Week Two
Wisdom and Finance 19

Week Three
Cultivating Contentment 31

Week Four
Defined by Generosity 43

Week Five (optional, no video)
Epilogue: Living the Good Life 55

HOW TO USE THIS LEADER GUIDE

Enough is a video-based study that explores what the Bible teaches us about financial management. Its purpose is to help participants get off of the consumerism treadmill and find the joy and contentment that come with a simpler and more generous way of living. Participants will assess their financial situation and develop a financial plan with a biblical foundation. This four-week study plus epilogue is appropriate for Sunday school classes, study groups, and others desiring to become wise stewards of the resources God has given them. As group leader, your role will be to facilitate the weekly sessions using this leader guide and the accompanying DVD.

A QUICK OVERVIEW

Because no two groups are alike, this guide has been designed to give you flexibility and choice in tailoring the sessions for your group. You may choose one of the following format options, or adapt these as you wish to meet the schedule and needs of your particular group.

(*Note*: The times indicated within parentheses are merely estimates. You may move at a faster or slower pace, making adjustments as necessary to stay on schedule.)

Basic Option: 60 minutes
Opening Prayer (2 minutes)
Biblical Foundation (3 minutes)
Video Presentation (15-20 minutes)
Group Discussion (25-30 minutes)
Taking It to Heart This Week (5 minutes)
Closing Prayer (<5 minutes)

Extended Option: 90 minutes
Opening Prayer (2 minutes)
Biblical Foundation (3 minutes)
Opening Activity (10-15 minutes)
Video Presentation (15-20 minutes)
Group Discussion (25-30 minutes)
Group Activity (15 minutes)
Taking It to Heart This Week (5 minutes)
Closing Prayer (<5 minutes)

Although you are encouraged to adapt the sessions to meet your needs, you also are encouraged to make prayer and Scripture regular components of the weekly group sessions. Feel free to use the opening and closing prayers provided or create your own prayers. In either case, the intent is to "cover" the group session in prayer, acknowledging that we are incapable of becoming wise stewards of our resources apart from God's grace and help. Likewise, the Scripture verses provided for each group session are intended to provide a biblical foundation for the group session as well as for participants' continuing reflection and application during the week.

In addition to the components outlined above, the following "leader helps" are provided to equip you for each group session:

Main Idea (session theme)
Session Goals (objectives for the group session)
Key Insights (summary of main points from the video)
Leader Extra (additional information related to the topic)
Notable Quote (noteworthy quote from the video)

You may use these helps for your personal preparation only, or you may choose to incorporate them into the group session in some way. For example, you might choose to write the main idea and/or session goals on a board or chart prior to the beginning of class, review the key insights from the video either before or after group discussion, incorporate the leader extra into group discussion, and close with the notable quote.

In addition to the materials provided for each group session, you will find a participant handout (which you may photocopy for participant use) at the end of each session. This handout includes a summary of the key insights from the video as well as "Taking It to Heart This Week" application exercises for the coming week. Remind participants that these exercises are designed to help them get the most out of this study that they possibly can. They alone are the ones who will determine whether or not this is just another group study or a transformational experience that will have a lasting, positive impact on their lives.

For groups that want to extend this four-week study to five weeks, an optional fifth session is provided based on the book's epilogue. This optional fifth session does not have a video.

CONTENTMENT PRAYER

Lord, help me be grateful for
what I have, remember that
I don't need most of what I want,
and that joy is found
in simplicity and generosity.

WEEK ONE

WHEN DREAMS BECOME NIGHTMARES

Main Idea: God's vision of financial management brings joy that the American Dream never can and never will bring.

GETTING STARTED

Session Goals

This session is intended to help participants:

- consider ways in which the American Dream has become an American nightmare
- understand *affluenza* and *credit-itis* and why they are dangerous
- learn how our sin nature affects our yearning for more
- consider how a changed heart can lead to changed desires

- discover the connection between simplicity and financial and spiritual freedom

Opening Prayer

Dear God, the topic of personal finances is a challenging one for many of us. We struggle with unwise spending decisions, rising credit card debt, and dwindling savings. We wrestle with the desire for more stuff, newer stuff, and better stuff. We resist the call to simplify and give more generously. Open our hearts to receive your wisdom and guidance, and empower us to respond by applying what we learn in practical ways so that we may become wise managers of our money and possessions. Amen.

Biblical Foundation

Some people, eager for money, have wandered from the faith and pierced themselves with many griefs.

(1 Timothy 6:10b, NIV)

The lover of money will not be satisfied with money; nor the lover of wealth, with gain. This also is vanity.

(Ecclesiastes 5:10)

For what will it profit them if they gain the whole world but forfeit their life? Or what will they give in return for their life?

(Matthew 16:26)

Opening Activity

Read aloud the excerpt from Alexis de Tocqueville's *Democracy in America* (see Leader Extra: de Tocqueville's Observation of Americans).

Consider how de Tocqueville's words, penned more than 160 years ago, are still descriptive of our nation today.

Ask:

- What are some ways we are "eager in the pursuit of immediate material pleasures"? List responses on a board or chart.

Discuss:

- Would you agree that the love of money is a primary or secondary motive behind most of what Americans do today? Why or why not?

LEARNING TOGETHER

Video Presentation

Play the DVD segment for Week 1, "When Dreams Become Nightmares."
Running Time: 15:24

Key Insights

1. We live in a world that encourages us to live beyond our means rather than be good stewards of our God-given resources.
2. When it comes to material possessions and money, we are not in a position to pass judgment on others, for we do not know their hearts.
3. For many people, the American Dream is a subconscious desire for achieving success and satisfying the desire for material possessions. Generally, it has come to mean consuming, acquiring, and buying.

4. We are affected socially and spiritually by two "illnesses" or conditions: affluenza and credit-itis. *Affluenza* is the constant need for more and bigger and better stuff. *Credit-itis* is the idea that we can have something now and pay for it later, which exploits our lack of self-discipline and allows us to feed our affluenza.
5. Most Americans spend money with very little self-discipline, saving less and spending more and more on credit.
6. A spiritual issue lies beneath the surface of our financial sickness: We have surrendered to the sin nature within us.
7. The starting point of the solution to our problem is a changed heart, which results in changed desires and a changed sense of life purpose.
8. As we allow Christ to work in us, seeking first his kingdom and striving to do his will, we begin to sense a higher calling to simplicity, faithfulness, and generosity.

Leader Extra: de Tocqueville's Observation of Americans

Alexis de Tocqueville (1805–1859) was a French political philosopher and historian of the nineteenth century. After traveling in the United States, he wrote *Democracy in America* (1835), which today is known as his major work and considered an early work of sociology and political science. In it, he offers this observation:

> [Americans] are extremely eager in the pursuit of immediate material pleasures and are always discontented with the position that they occupy. . . . They think about nothing but ways of changing their lot and bettering it. For people in this frame of mind every new way of getting wealth more quickly, every machine which lessens work, every means of diminishing the cost of production, every invention which makes pleasures easier or greater, seems the most magnificent

The Farmer's Dog
Get 60% Off Fresh, Healthy Dog Food
Say goodbye to ultra-processed kibble and hello to *real* food.
THEFARMERSDOG.COM/PRIVACY
The Farmer's Dog
Buddy's
Turkey Recipe
Feed Buddy
½ pack per day
daily
Sent with ♥ on Mar 28
Keeps in fridge for 4 days after thawing
Stores in freezer up to 6 months
Questions? Text or call (646) 780-7957
Scan for feeding tips!
#LongLiveDogs

> accomplishment of the human mind. . . . One usually finds that the love of money is either the chief or a secondary motive at the bottom of everything the Americans do. This gives a family likeness to all their passions and soon makes them wearisome to contemplate.*

Group Discussion

1. What are some ways the world encourages us to live beyond our means? What challenges do you face when trying to save and be a good steward of your God-given resources?
2. Why is it dangerous to pass judgment on others regarding the way they spend their money? Read Matthew 7:1-5. What can we learn from these verses?
3. How do you think most people would describe or define the "American Dream"? How does this dream contrast with other "dreams" throughout our nation's history? How can this dream become a nightmare for people?
4. *(Skip this question if you did the Opening Activity.)* Read and discuss the Leader Extra: de Tocqueville's Observation of Americans. What are some ways we are "eager in the pursuit of immediate material pleasures"? Would you agree that the love of money is a primary or secondary motive behind most of what Americans do today? Why or why not?
5. In what ways do you struggle with affluenza and credit-itis? How are these "conditions" a problem for us as individuals, as families, and as a nation?
6. How do marketing and advertising campaigns fuel our yearning for more? What are some of the manipulative messages advertisers convey in order to get us to buy their products?

---

* Alexis de Tocqueville, *Democracy in America and Two Essays on America* (London: Penguin, 2003), 534, 713.

7. What are the root causes of our continual yearning for more? How is sin a part of the problem?
8. What role do you think God wants money and possessions to play in our lives?
9. How is a changed heart the starting point to the solution of our problem with money and possessions? How is this heart change both a one-time event and an ongoing transformation?
10. How has this discussion helped or challenged you?

Group Activity

The author suggests that as we allow Christ to work in us, we begin to sense a higher calling to simplicity and generosity. Have the group share responses to this question:

- If you were free from debt, how might you be able to use your resources to make a difference in the lives of others?

Write the responses on a large sheet of chart paper and post it in the room for the duration of the study as a reminder of the Kingdom work God can accomplish through those who learn to mange their resources wisely.

WRAPPING UP

Taking It to Heart This Week

Explain that there are two resources available to help participants with personal application each week. First, there is the Participant Handout, which includes application activities participants may complete at home. Participants will receive a handout at the conclusion of the group session for weeks 1–4. Explain that these activities are for personal use only and will not be shared with the group. Their purpose is to help participants get the most out of this study that they possibly can.

Second, there is the book *Enough* by Adam Hamilton. The video segments of this study bring together the main themes of the book. Those who read the book will be better prepared to participate in group discussions and activities. Invite those participants who have already purchased copies of the book to read Chapter 1 this week, if they have not already done so. They may choose to read Chapter 2 as well, if they like, in preparation for next week's session. Those participants who have not ordered/purchased copies of the book will want to do so now.

Notable Quote

> *"God has a plan for your life, and part of [this plan] is that you are fruitful, that you have a chance to do his kingdom work, and that you live into his will for your life. But our spiritual lives remain immature and unfruitful as long as we're pursuing the American Dream as the culture tells us to."*
>
> —*Adam Hamilton*

Closing Prayer

Lord, we confess that in many ways we have bought into the lie of the "American Dream," which says that success is defined by profits, portfolios, possessions, prestige, and pleasure. We struggle with the yearning for more, and often we try to satisfy this yearning by pursuing material things rather than pursuing you. Forgive us, Lord. Change our hearts, and correct our vision. Give us your perspective on money and possessions. Help us not to focus on all the things we wish we had, but to be grateful for what we do have. Teach us to wisely manage the resources you have given us so that when you prompt us to help those in need, we are free to do it. Enable us to live simply, to be content, and to give generously. Amen.

WEEK 1: WHEN DREAMS BECOME NIGHTMARES PARTICIPANT HANDOUT

Some people, eager for money, have wandered from the faith and pierced themselves with many griefs.

(1 Timothy 6:10b, NIV)

Key Insights

1. We live in a world that encourages us to live beyond our means rather than be good stewards of our God-given resources.
2. When it comes to material possessions and money, we are not in a position to pass judgment on others, for we do not know their hearts.
3. For many people, the American Dream is a subconscious desire for achieving success and satisfying the desire for material possessions. Generally, it has come to mean consuming, acquiring, and buying.
4. We are affected socially and spiritually by two "illnesses" or conditions: affluenza and credit-itis. *Affluenza* is the constant need for more and bigger and better stuff. *Credit-itis* is the idea that we can have something now and pay for it later, which exploits our lack of self-discipline and allows us to feed our affluenza.
5. Most Americans spend money with very little self-discipline, saving less and spending more and more on credit.
6. A spiritual issue lies beneath the surface of our financial sickness: We have surrendered to the sin nature within us.
7. The starting point of the solution to our problem is a changed heart, which results in changed desires and a changed sense of life purpose.

8. As we allow Christ to work in us, seeking first his kingdom and striving to do his will, we begin to sense a higher calling to simplicity, faithfulness, and generosity.

Taking It to Heart This Week

- Look ahead to next week's chapter, "Wisdom and Finance," and complete the Budget Worksheet at the end of the chapter.
- Choose one type of expense to track this week.

WEEK TWO

WISDOM AND FINANCE

Main Idea: Biblical wisdom and basic money management principles are essential if we are to achieve financial peace and accomplish God's greater purposes for our lives.

GETTING STARTED

Session Goals

This session is intended to help participants:

- look closely at biblical principles of money management and learn how to apply them to their lives
- review common financial pitfalls and cultural traps and learn how to avoid them
- think about their life purpose—their vision, mission, and calling
- set goals that will enable them to utilize their resources in ways that are consistent with their life purpose

- develop a plan utilizing six basic financial planning principles
- consider how simplifying their lives can help them to get their finances in order and devote more of their resources to fulfilling God's calling

Opening Prayer

O God, we desperately need your guidance and instruction in order to become the wise money managers you desire us to be. We come today seeking your wisdom and your counsel. Open our eyes so that we may recognize the cultural traps we have fallen into. Teach us how to avoid the financial pitfalls that derail us from the path you would have us to walk. Lead us in setting goals and developing plans that will enable us to achieve financial peace and accomplish the greater purposes you have for our lives. In Jesus' name we pray. Amen.

Biblical Foundation

The plans of the diligent lead surely to abundance,
but everyone who is hasty comes only to want.
(Proverbs 21:5)

Precious treasure remains in the house of the wise,
but the fool devours it.
(Proverbs 21:20)

Opening Activity

Read aloud the following excerpt from *Enough*:

> We live in a time of excessive materialism. Many people today are on a treadmill of consumerism, and that treadmill

just keeps going faster and faster. But the day will come when either we are going to break down or the treadmill is going to break down, because we cannot continue to go faster and faster in our passion to consume.

Discuss:

- In what ways are we on a treadmill of consumerism—as individuals, as families, and as a nation?
- How many are 1 tragedy away from disaster?

Write responses on a board or chart, saving them for the group activity later in the session.

LEARNING TOGETHER

Video Presentation

Play the DVD segment for Week 2, "Wisdom and Finance."
Running Time: 18:30

Key Insights

1. Many of us have a bit of the prodigal son in us: We have the habits of squandering and wasting money.
2. As human beings, we have a tendency to focus on today rather than plan for tomorrow.
3. When our life purpose is having as much pleasure as we can in the moment, the things we do tend to become less and less satisfying until finally we come to a place where we're entirely dissatisfied—and often broke.
4. Two of the primary money-wasters we struggle with are impulse buying and eating out.

5. The rule-of-thumb regarding impulse buys is to shop for what you need only. Make a list, buy what you need, and get out of the store. If this is difficult, wait twenty-four hours before purchasing an impulse buy.
6. Society tells us that our life purpose is to consume; the Bible tells us that our life purpose is to love God and to love our neighbors as ourselves. Our money and possessions should be devoted to helping us fulfill this calling.
7. Being able to accomplish the greater purposes God has for our lives requires goal setting and planning.
8. Without a plan to reach our goals, we will revert to being prodigals. A plan gives us concrete steps that we can take to accomplish our goals.
9. Six financial planning principles can help us to become better money managers:
    - Pay your tithe and offering *first.*
    - Create a budget and track your expenses.
    - Simplify your lifestyle (live below your means).
    - Establish an emergency fund.
    - Pay off your credit cards, use cash/debit cards for purchases, and use credit wisely.
    - Practice long-term savings and investing habits.
10. Simplifying our lives enables us to give more generously and experience the joy that comes from living for something beyond ourselves.

Leader Extra: Three Types of Savings

Saving money is the number one wise money management principle everyone should practice. There are three types of savings we should have.

1. *Emergency savings* is an account separate from checking or long-term savings that is set aside specifically for emergencies.

2. *Saving for wants and goals* is setting aside money in advance for things we know we will need or want, rather than buying them on credit. For larger savings goals, routinely deduct a percentage from your paycheck and deposit this amount in a savings account or investment option. Set up a direct deposit so that the money is automatically deducted from your paycheck and deposited into the appropriate account. Do not have a debit card on your savings account, and do not link your savings account to your checking account.

3. *Retirement savings* accumulated throughout your career is a way to take advantage of the power of interest over time. Here is one retirement savings plan that begins at age eighteen: Set aside $25 per month for retirement, increasing that amount each year by $25 per month while in college. Upon graduation, add an additional $100 per month to this fund, bringing the total to $200 per month. If you do not go to college and begin working full-time out of high school, or if you are already in the workforce now, start saving $200 per month if possible. If you were to follow this plan from age eighteen until retirement, carefully investing the money in a ROTH Individual Retirement Account, you would have over one million dollars at retirement.

Leader Extra: Budget Percentage Recommendations

When creating a budget, it is helpful to determine what percentage of your income you plan to spend in each category. Here are some recommended percentages for common budgetary categories:

Item	*Suggested %**
Housing	25-35%
Transportation	10-15%
Charitable Gifts	10-12%
Food	5-15%
Saving	5-10%
Utilities	5-10%
Medical/Health	5-10%
Debt	5-10%
Clothing	2-7%
Personal/Miscellaneous	12-23%

Group Discussion

1. Which of the following questions resonates more with you right now, and why?
   - Are you heading toward a looming financial crisis?
   - Are you wasting what you have, spending money here and there because you can afford to?
2. Read Luke 15:11-16. In what ways are we like the prodigal son? What are some of the ways we squander our money and resources?
3. Why do you think we are inclined to focus on the moment rather than think about and plan for tomorrow? What is the danger in this kind of attitude?
4. The author identifies two common money-wasters: impulse buying and eating out. Which of these money-wasters is more problematic for you and why? What are some other ways you tend to waste money or resources? What are some ways you might address these money-wasters?

---

* These percentages are adapted from Dave Ramsey's *The Total Money Makeover* (Nashville: Thomas Nelson, 2007).

5. What does society tell us about our life purpose? What does the Bible tell us about our life purpose?
6. How would you describe *your* life purpose—your vision or mission or calling? Why is your understanding of your life purpose important to the way you handle your finances? What does the phrase "blessed to be a blessing" mean to you?
7. How can goals and plans help us to accomplish the greater purposes God has for our lives? What happens when we do not have goals and plans?
8. Review and discuss the six financial planning principles (see Key Insights). Which principles are more challenging for you, and why? What would help you to implement or improve these principles in your life?
9. Why are creating a budget and tracking expenses critical to wise money management? Review the recommended percentages for budgetary categories (see Leader Extra: Budget Percentage Recommendations). Do any of these recommended percentages surprise you, and if so, why? Are there other categories you would include in your budget, and how might you determine an appropriate percentage for these categories?
10. Discuss the three types of savings (see Leader Extra: Three Types of Savings) and why each is important to financial peace and well-being.
11. If we want to achieve financial peace and accomplish God's greater purposes for our lives, what are our only two options? Why is simplifying our lives a more viable option? What does the phrase "simplifying your lifestyle" mean to you? How would you explain this concept to someone else?
12. How has this discussion helped or challenged you?

Group Activity

Review the comments generated in the Opening Activity. Then brainstorm solutions—practical ideas that can help us to "get off the consumerism treadmill." Write these on a board or chart. Challenge participants to choose one or two ideas they can begin to implement in their homes, workplaces, and neighborhoods/communities this week.

WRAPPING UP

Taking It to Heart This Week

Briefly review the Taking It to Heart This Week application exercises included in the Participant Handout. Encourage participants to complete the activities during the coming week. Remind participants to continue reading the next chapter in the book *Enough*.

Notable Quote

> *"To be a Christian is to follow Jesus Christ and to seek to do his will in our lives. It is to say, 'Here I am, all of me! I'm yours. Put me to work, help me to serve, use me to accomplish your work.' Now, if this is our life purpose, then our money and possessions should be devoted to helping us fulfill this calling. . . . We are blessed to be a blessing."*
>
> —*Adam Hamilton*

Closing Prayer

Generous God, all we have comes from you, yet we are not always wise stewards of what you have so graciously given us. We have listened to the lure of the world, buying and consuming compulsively and excessively. Forgive us for being wasteful like the prodigal son.

Forgive us for leveraging our future in order to have pleasure in the present. As we leave here today, help us begin to put into practice the biblical and practical wisdom we have discussed so that we may become good managers of all you have given us. Teach us to be generous and willing to share—to be Kingdom-minded people who are focused on accomplishing your purposes for our lives. Amen.

WEEK 2: WISDOM AND FINANCE PARTICIPANT HANDOUT

The plans of the diligent lead surely to abundance,
but everyone who is hasty comes only to want.
(Proverbs 21:5)

Key Insights

1. Many of us have a bit of the prodigal son in us: We have the habits of squandering and wasting money.
2. As human beings, we have a tendency to focus on today rather than plan for tomorrow.
3. When our life purpose is having as much pleasure as we can in the moment, the things we do tend to become less and less satisfying until finally we come to a place where we're entirely dissatisfied—and often broke.
4. Two of the primary money-wasters we struggle with are impulse buying and eating out.
5. The rule-of-thumb regarding impulse buys is to shop for what you need only. Make a list, buy what you need, and get out of the store. If this is difficult, wait twenty-four hours before purchasing an impulse buy.
6. Society tells us that our life purpose is to consume; the Bible tells us that our life purpose is to love God and to love our neighbors as ourselves. Our money and possessions should be devoted to helping us fulfill this calling.
7. Being able to accomplish the greater purposes God has for our lives requires goal setting and planning.
8. Without a plan to reach our goals, we will revert to being prodigals. A plan gives us concrete steps that we can take to accomplish our goals.

9. Six financial planning principles can help us to become better money managers:
    - Pay your tithe and offering *first*.
    - Create a budget and track your expenses.
    - Simplify your lifestyle (live below your means).
    - Establish an emergency fund.
    - Pay off your credit cards, use cash/debit cards for purchases, and use credit wisely.
    - Practice long-term savings and investing habits.
10. Simplifying our lives enables us to give more generously and experience the joy that comes from living for something beyond ourselves.

Taking It to Heart This Week

- Complete the questions in Reflecting on the Six Financial Planning Principles (found at the end of *Enough*).

WEEK THREE

CULTIVATING CONTENTMENT

Main Idea: Our lives do not consist in the abundance of possessions.

GETTING STARTED

Session Goals

This session is intended to help participants:

- remember that life does not consist in the abundance of possessions
- explore the underlying reason for our discontent
- consider four keys to cultivating contentment
- embrace five steps for simplifying their lives
- understand the power of self-control
- consciously choose contentment

Opening Prayer

Dear God, you have wired our hearts so that we long for you, yet so often we try to satisfy this longing with other things. Forgive us, Lord. Teach us to find our true satisfaction in you alone. Give us wisdom and understanding so that we may learn how to cultivate contentment in our lives. Fill our minds and hearts with truth and the power of self-control so that we may stand firm against the temptation to seek instant gratification, choosing instead a higher and greater good. In Jesus' name we pray. Amen.

Biblical Foundation

Keep your lives free from the love of money, and be content with what you have; for he has said, "I will never leave you or forsake you." So we can say with confidence,

"The Lord is my helper;
I will not be afraid."

(Hebrews 13:5-6)

And [Jesus] said to them, "Take care! Be on your guard against all kinds of greed; for one's life does not consist in the abundance of possessions."

(Luke 12:15)

Whatever my eyes desired I did not keep from them; I kept my heart from no pleasure. . . . Then I considered all that my hands had done and the toil I had spent in doing it, and again, all was vanity and a chasing after wind.

(Ecclesiastes 2:10-11)

Opening Activity

Invite participants to respond in popcorn fashion to the following questions:

- What things in your life are you discontent with (dissatisfied with)?
- What things in your life are you content with (satisfied with)?

Write the responses in two lists on a board or chart, giving each column a heading. Briefly discuss:

- Do you believe God wants us to be content or satisfied with everything in our lives? Why or why not?

Now create two new lists by having participants answer these revised questions:

- What things in your life do you think God wants you to be content with?
- What things in your life do you think God wants you to be discontent with?

Note how these new lists compare to the previous lists.

LEARNING TOGETHER

Video Presentation

Play the DVD segment for Week 3, "Cultivating Contentment."
Running Time 19:00

Key Insights

1. Although Jesus tells us that our lives consist of more than the abundance of possessions, the culture shouts it's not true. The result is a wrestling in our hearts.
2. We suffer from Restless Heart Syndrome (RHS)—we are never satisfied with anything but are perennially discontent. If left unchecked, RHS can destroy us.
3. God wired our hearts so that they would be content with certain things and discontent with others, causing us to seek the only One who can fully satisfy us. The problem is that we tend to be discontent with the wrong things.
4. Like the apostle Paul, we can learn to be content in whatever circumstances we may find ourselves. Four keys to contentment can help us to do this:
    - Remember that it could be worse.
    - Ask yourself, "How long will this make me happy?"
    - Develop a grateful heart.
    - Ask yourself, "Where does my soul find true satisfaction?"
5. Gratitude is essential if we are to be content. Expressing gratitude to God changes our hearts.
6. Contrary to what the world would have us believe, the longings of our souls are satisfied only in God.
7. Contentment and simplicity go hand in hand. When we simplify, we are content; and when we are content, we simplify.
8. Five steps can help us to simplify our lives:
    - Reduce your consumption and live below your means.
    - Before making a purchase, ask yourself why you need it and want it.
    - Use something up before buying something new.
    - Plan low-cost entertainment that enriches.
    - Consider major changes that would allow you to simplify your life.

9. Simplifying our lives requires self-control. Self-control protects us from temptation and from sins that can destroy us. Self-control is choosing delayed gratification for a higher cause rather than satisfying an impulse for instant gratification.
10. Choosing contentment does not mean that we must stop buying things; it means we look to God as our Source and reclaim the joy of generosity and simplicity.

Leader Extra: Scriptures on Contentment and the Source of Our True Satisfaction

O God, you are my God, I seek you,
my soul thirsts for you. . . .
My soul is satisfied as with a rich feast,
and my mouth praises you with joyful lips
when I think of you on my bed,
and meditate on you in the watches of the night.
(Psalm 63:1, 5-6)

I have learned to be content with whatever I have. I know what it is to have little, and I know what it is to have plenty. In any and all circumstances I have learned the secret of being well-fed and of going hungry, of having plenty and of being in need. I can do all things through [Christ] who strengthens me.
(Philippians 4:11-13)

Leader Extra: Consequences of Our Consuming Habits

Our consuming habits have serious consequences that affect not only our personal and national debt, but also our world. Consider these statistics:

- Every year Americans consume over 1.2 billion trees to support our needs for packaging, paper, napkins, and bags.
- We use 2,500,000 plastic bottles every hour—most of these for *water.*
- We represent only 5 percent of the world's population, yet we produce 40 percent of the world's garbage—an average of 1,609 pounds per person per year.*

These consuming habits are not only wasteful; they are unsustainable. If the rate of our consumption continues to increase each year, it soon will outpace the growth of the population. We cannot continue this trend and think that everything will be okay. Eventually, we will exceed the rate at which resources can be renewed.

Group Discussion

1. If a tornado was headed toward your home and you had ten minutes to grab whatever you could before heading to the basement, what would you take with you?
2. Read Luke 12:15. How do Jesus' words contradict the messages of the world? Why do you think so many Christians struggle to live according to the truth of Luke 12:15? What can help us?
3. How would you explain Restless Heart Syndrome (RHS)? In what ways can it harm us?
4. Why do you think we tend to be discontent with the things God wants us to be content with, and vice versa? What are some of the results of our discontent?
5. Review the four keys to cultivating contentment. Which of these ideas do you think would be most helpful or effective to you personally, and why?

---

* These statistics are from Recycling-Revolution.com; http://www.recycling-revolution.com/recycling-facts.html.

6. Are you a person who tends to see the glass half full or half empty? How can finding something good to focus on in every circumstance help us to be more content?
7. Why do you think things only bring us temporary happiness and satisfaction? When has the concept of "try before you buy" proven helpful to you?
8. Read 1 Thessalonians 5:18. What significance does the word *in* have in this verse? How does expressing gratitude to God—even before we *feel* thankful—change us?
9. Read the verses found in Leader Extra: Scriptures on Contentment and the Source of Our True Satisfaction. What do these verses tell us about the source of our true satisfaction?
10. Reread Philippians 4:11-13. What was Paul's "secret" to contentment? Describe a time when you discovered, like Paul, that your deepest needs are satisfied in your relationship with God through Christ.
11. How is simplifying our lives beneficial to us—personally, nationally, and globally?
12. Review and discuss the five steps to simplifying your life. Which step do you think might bring the greatest results for you/your family, and why?
13. Read Proverbs 25:28. What does this verse teach us about self-control? How can self-control help us to simplify our lives and increase our contentment?
14. How has this discussion helped or challenged you?

Group Activity

Read aloud Leader Extra: Consequences of Our Consuming Habits. Brainstorm ways we can reduce our consumption and save money and resources—as individuals, families, companies, communities, and the church. Work together or break into small groups, assigning each group a different category or area. Recruit a volunteer (or one per group) to record the ideas. Before the next group session, email the list to participants.

WRAPPING UP

Taking It to Heart This Week

Briefly review the Taking It to Heart This Week application exercises included in the Participant Handout. Encourage participants to complete the activities during the coming week. Remind participants to continue reading the next chapter in *Enough*.

Notable Quote

> *"Contentment is found in our relationship with God and our relationships with others. This is why Jesus said the two most important things we must do are to 'love the Lord your God with all your heart, and with all your soul, and with all your mind,' and to 'love your neighbor as yourself' (Matthew 22:37, 39). If we keep our focus on these two things, we will find satisfaction for our souls and lasting contentment."*
>
> —*Adam Hamilton*

Closing Prayer

Lord, cure us of restless heart syndrome. We are truly sorry for the times when we have been ungrateful for the gifts you have given us—unsatisfied with our spouse, unsatisfied with our children or our parents, unsatisfied with our homes or our cars or our healthcare or our jobs. Forgive us for offending you with our discontent, and forgive us for being content with things we are not supposed to be content with. Help us to have a deep longing for you and your will for our lives. Give us the desire to pursue righteousness, holiness, justice, and love. Help us to simplify our lives, and to find our peace in you. We ask these mercies in your holy name. Amen.

WEEK 3:
CULTIVATING CONTENTMENT
PARTICIPANT HANDOUT

[Jesus] said to them, "Take care! Be on your guard against all kinds of greed; for one's life does not consist in the abundance of possessions."

(Luke 12:15)

Key Insights

1. Although Jesus tells us that our lives consist of more than the abundance of possessions, the culture shouts it's not true. The result is a wrestling in our hearts.
2. We suffer from Restless Heart Syndrome (RHS)—we are never satisfied with anything but are perennially discontent. If left unchecked, RHS can destroy us.
3. God wired our hearts so that they would be content with certain things and discontent with others, causing us to seek the only One who can fully satisfy us. The problem is that we tend to be discontent with the wrong things.
4. Like the apostle Paul, we can learn to be content in whatever circumstances we may find ourselves. Four keys to contentment can help us to do this:
    - Remember that it could be worse.
    - Ask yourself, "How long will this make me happy?"
    - Develop a grateful heart.
    - Ask yourself, "Where does my soul find true satisfaction?"
5. Gratitude is essential if we are to be content. Expressing gratitude to God changes our hearts.
6. Contrary to what the world would have us believe, the longings of our souls are satisfied only in God.

7. Contentment and simplicity go hand in hand. When we simplify, we are content; and when we are content, we simplify.
8. Five steps can help us to simplify our lives:
   - Reduce your consumption and live below your means.
   - Before making a purchase, ask yourself why you need it and want it.
   - Use something up before buying something new.
   - Plan low-cost entertainment that enriches.
   - Consider major changes that would allow you to simplify your life.
9. Simplifying our lives requires self-control. Self-control protects us from temptation and from sins that can destroy us. Self-control is choosing delayed gratification for a higher cause rather than satisfying an impulse for instant gratification.
10. Choosing contentment does not mean that we must stop buying things; it means we look to God as our Source and reclaim the joy of generosity and simplicity.

Taking It to Heart This Week

- Review the four keys to cultivating contentment (found in *Enough* Chapter 3). Make a point to practice each of these in the coming week.
- Consider the five steps for simplifying your life (found in *Enough* Chapter 3). How can you apply each of these in your life *now*?

WEEK FOUR

DEFINED BY GENEROSITY

Main Idea: We experience true joy when our lives are defined by generosity.

GETTING STARTED

Session Goals

This session is intended to help participants:

- realize that we were created to be generous
- understand how to defeat the voices of fear and self-gratification
- recognize that their lives are not their own
- explore a theological foundation for generosity
- understand and strive toward tithing and giving offerings beyond the tithe

- recognize the outcomes of our generosity—for ourselves, for others, and for God

Opening Prayer

Dear God, you designed us to be generous. You actually gave us the need to be generous, which is why we experience such joy when we give selflessly and sacrificially to you and to others. Forgive us for listening to the voices of the world that tell us we need to focus on ourselves rather than on others. Forgive us for choosing to hoard rather than to give. Forgive us for giving in to self-gratification rather than practicing delayed gratification. Teach us, Lord, to give generously of all you have so graciously given to us, so that we may bless both you and others and experience the abundant blessings that come from living for you. Amen.

Biblical Foundation

As for those who in the present age are rich, command them not to be haughty, or to set their hopes on the uncertainty of riches, but rather on God who richly provides us with everything for our enjoyment. They are to do good, to be rich in good works, generous, and ready to share, thus storing up for themselves the treasure of a good foundation for the future, so that they may take hold of the life that really is life.

(1 Timothy 6:17-19)

Some give freely, yet grow all the richer;
others withhold what is due, and only suffer want.
A generous person will be enriched,
and one who gives water will get water.

(Proverbs 11:24-25)

Those who are generous are blessed,
for they share their bread with the poor.
(Proverbs 22:9)

Opening Activity

Read aloud the following excerpt from *Enough*:

> As the Holy Spirit continues to work in our lives, we begin to think less about ourselves and more about others. We begin to see the needs of others and wonder, *If I don't do something, who will?* As this change takes place within us, we experience real joy. We discover that we find more joy in doing things for other people and for God than we ever did in doing things for ourselves. This is what Jesus meant when he said, "It is more blessed to give than to receive" (Acts 20:35). In the very act of losing our lives, we find life, just as Jesus said, "For those who want to save their life will lose it, and those who lose their life for my sake will find it" (Matthew 16:25).

Invite each participant to tell briefly of a time when he or she discovered real joy by giving selflessly of his or her time, talents, or resources. (If your group is large, divide into small groups for sharing.) Discuss:

- How do we "gain" more than we "lose" when we give generously to others?

LEARNING TOGETHER

Video Presentation

Play the DVD segment for Week 4, "Defined by Generosity."
Running Time 18:55

Key Insights

1. God designed us to be generous.
2. There are two "voices" that war against our God-given impulse toward generosity: fear and self-gratification. As we put our faith in Jesus Christ and grow spiritually, we silence these voices and become more and more generous.
3. As we realize that our lives are not our own, we are willing to give more generously and make sacrifices because we know our security is in God. As this change takes place within us, we discover real joy.
4. A central theological foundation for generosity is this: *Life is a gift, and everything belongs to God.*
5. From the earliest biblical times, the primary way people worshiped God was building an altar and offering the fruit of their labors upon it to God. In Old Testament times, a gift offered to God was called the *first fruits* or the *tithe,* and it equaled one-tenth of one's flocks or crops or income.
6. Most Christians agree that the tithe is still a good guideline for our lives today, and one that is pleasing to God.
7. We who are blessed with more than enough to meet our needs should consider giving beyond the tithe.
8. The Lord is pleased when we give freely with grateful hearts. When offered in pure, selfless love, our offerings bless the Lord.
9. Our generosity to God and others not only blesses God and other people; it also changes us, filling our lives with joy.
10. We do not give to God so that we can get something in return. Yet when we give to God and to others, the blessings just seem to come back to us.

Leader Extra: Wesleyan Covenant Prayer

I am no longer my own, but thine.
Put me to what thou wilt, rank me with whom thou wilt.
Put me to doing, put me to suffering.
Let me be employed for thee or laid aside for thee,
Exalted for thee or brought low for thee.
Let me be full, let me be empty.
Let me have all things, let me have nothing.
I freely and heartily yield all things
to thy pleasure and disposal. . . . Amen. *

Leader Extra: A Biblical History of Tithing

From the early days of the Old Testament, God's people observed the practice of giving some portion of the best of what they had to God. In the beginning, the practice was to burn these offerings completely, saving no portion of the offering for food for themselves or others. This was a way of saying, "God, I give this to you, and it's all yours." In later times, the people would bring their offerings to the priests and offer them to God for the work of the temple and the priesthood. A gift offered to God was called the *first fruits* or the *tithe,* and it equaled one-tenth of one's flocks or crops or income. Abraham was the first to give a tithe or tenth. After victory in battle, Abraham took 10 percent of the spoils of war and gave them to the priest-king Melchizedek for God's glory (Genesis 14:17-24). Abraham's grandson, Jacob, whose name also was Israel, made a covenant with God that included giving one-tenth of all he had to God. He said:

"If God will be with me, and will keep me in this way that I go, and will give me bread to eat and clothing to wear, so that I come again

* From "A Covenant Prayer in the Wesleyan Tradition," in *The United Methodist Hymnal* (Nashville: The United Methodist Publishing House, 1989), 607.

to my father's house in peace, then the LORD *shall be my God, and this stone, which I have set up for a pillar, shall be God's house; and of all that you give me I will surely give one-tenth to you."*

(Genesis 28:20-22)

In the time of Moses, the tithe was codified in the law. God claimed one-tenth of the best the people had. Before giving to the poor and taking care of themselves, they were to bring one-tenth of their first fruits to God. Leviticus 27:30 says, "All tithes from the land, whether the seed from the ground or the fruit from the tree, are the LORD's; they are holy to the LORD." Whether it was the produce of the ground or the offspring of the flocks, the first tenth was holy to the Lord.

Group Discussion

1. If you were participating in a debate, how would you defend the following statement? *When God created humankind, God designed us to be generous.*
2. What are the two "voices" that war against our God-given impulse toward generosity? How do we defeat these voices, and what happens as we do?
3. What happens as we realize that our lives are not our own? What has helped you to come to this realization in your own life?
4. Read Acts 20:35 and Matthew 16:25. What does Jesus teach us about generosity in these verses?
5. Read Psalm 24:1. How does this verse inform or shape your thoughts about generosity? How might this one verse be foundational to a theology of generosity?
6. Read Leviticus 25:23. According to this verse, what is our "job description"? What does it mean to be stewards of the blessings of God?

7. Why do you think giving an offering was the central act of worship from the earliest biblical times? What was the significance of the first fruits or the tithe?
8. Do you think the giving of tithes and offerings is the central act of worship today? How might we reclaim the significance of this important act of worship?
9. In what ways do many Christians find the idea of tithing challenging? How might we overcome these challenges and begin to move toward the habit of tithing? Share from your own experience as you are willing.
10. Do you believe that tithing is possible from virtually any income level? Why or why not?
11. Read Luke 12:48. How does this verse support the idea that those who are blessed with more than enough to meet their needs should consider giving beyond the tithe?
12. Read Mark 12:41-44 and 2 Corinthians 9:7. According to these verses, what kind of offering pleases God? How does such an offering "bless" God?
13. How does our generosity not only change others but also change us? In what ways have you been changed by giving generously? How have your gifts "returned" to you as blessings?
14. How has this discussion helped or challenged you?

Group Activity

Use the Wesleyan Covenant Prayer (listed on p. 47) as a group prayer exercise. Invite participants to find a comfortable prayer posture. Give permission for them to sit, stand, kneel, or even lie prostrate (space permitting). Move chairs and tables as necessary and dim the lighting (you may need to bring candles to achieve the desired effect). If you desire, you may play quiet instrumental music in the background during the prayer. Avoid songs with lyrics so that participants are not distracted.

Explain that you will read one line of the prayer and then pause for approximately 60-90 seconds. (Use a watch with a second hand to keep time.) During this silent time, participants are to meditate on the phrase, asking God to speak to them. Be sure to wait 60-90 seconds before proceeding to the next line so that participants have time to meditate and listen for God.

WRAPPING UP

Taking It to Heart This Week

Briefly review the Taking It to Heart This Week application exercises included in the Participant Handout. Encourage participants to complete the activities during the coming week. Remind participants to continue reading the next chapter in *Enough*.

Notable Quote

> *"As the Holy Spirit continues to work in our lives, we begin to think less about ourselves and more about others. We begin to see the needs of others and wonder, If I don't do something, who will? As this change takes place within us, we experience real joy. We discover that we find more joy in doing things for other people and for God than we ever did in doing things for ourselves."*
>
> *—Adam Hamilton*

Closing Prayer

O God, we thank you that you have given us life, that you sustain us by the power of your Holy Spirit, and that you gave Jesus Christ as an offering for us and for our sins. We thank you for the abundance that we have in our lives. Help us, O Lord, to honor you with our tithes and care for the poor and those who are in need. Help us to recognize that it is more blessed to give than to receive. We offer ourselves to you. In Jesus' holy name we pray. Amen.

Opening question – How do we gain more than we lose when we generously give to others?

WEEK 4:
DEFINED BY GENEROSITY
PARTICIPANT HANDOUT

Some give freely, yet grow all the richer;
others withhold what is due, and only suffer want.
A generous person will be enriched,
and one who gives water will get water.
(Proverbs 11:24-25)

Key Insights

1. God designed us to be generous.
2. There are two "voices" that war against our God-given impulse toward generosity: fear and self-gratification. As we put our faith in Jesus Christ and grow spiritually, we silence these voices and become more and more generous.
3. As we realize that our lives are not our own, we are willing to give more generously and make sacrifices because we know our security is in God. As this change takes place within us, we discover real joy.
4. A central theological foundation for generosity is this: *Life is a gift, and everything belongs to God.*
5. From the earliest biblical times, the primary way people worshiped God was building an altar and offering the fruit of their labors upon it to God. In Old Testament times, a gift offered to God was called the *first fruits* or the *tithe,* and it equaled one-tenth of one's flocks or crops or income.
6. Most Christians agree that the tithe is still a good guideline for our lives today, and one that is pleasing to God.
7. We who are blessed with more than enough to meet our needs should consider giving beyond the tithe.

8. The Lord is pleased when we give freely with grateful hearts. When offered in pure, selfless love, our offerings bless the Lord.
9. Our generosity to God and others not only blesses God and other people; it also changes us, filling our lives with joy.
10. We do not give to God so that we can get something in return. Yet when we give to God and to others, the blessings just seem to come back to us.

Taking It to Heart This Week

- Over the next week, read the "Epilogue: Living the Good Life." Also review the Financial Management Assessment Tools at the end of *Enough*.

Conclusion - We experience true joy when our lives are defined by generosity!

WEEK FIVE
(OPTIONAL, NO VIDEO)

EPILOGUE: LIVING THE GOOD LIFE

Main Idea: We experience the rich, fulfilled life that God intended for us when we live in relationship with others and trust fully in God.

GETTING STARTED

Session Goals

This session is intended to help participants:

- understand that material possessions and career success are false pathways that do not lead us to the good life
- perceive how our society's emphasis on wealth and possessions has not produced more satisfaction, but less
- recognize that the good life God intends for us is defined by human flourishing and a sense of purpose and fulfillment

- understand the importance of investing in relationships over investing in things
- move toward a life characterized by working for the good of all
- develop a deeper trust in God that frees us from a life of worry and fear

Opening Prayer

Dear God, you said that you came into our world through Jesus so that we might have abundant life. But too often, we have chosen to define that life in terms of wealth and possessions—something you have repeatedly warned us against. Too often, we have rebelled against your love and put our own success over your call to love our neighbors. Too often, we have chosen to trust in ourselves to obtain what we think we want instead of trusting fully in you to provide what we need. Free our hearts and minds today to understand your Word for us, so that we may experience the fulfilled life you intend for us all. Amen.

Biblical Foundation

One of them, a lawyer, asked him a question to test him. "Teacher, which commandment in the law is the greatest?" He said to him, "'You shall love the Lord your God with all your heart, and with all your soul, and with all your mind.' This is the greatest and first commandment. And a second is like it: 'You shall love your neighbor as yourself.' On these two commandments hang all the law and the prophets."

(Matthew 22:35-40)

We know that we have passed from death to life because we love one another.

(1 John 3:14)

I trusted in your steadfast love;
my heart shall rejoice in your salvation.
I will sing to the L*ORD*,
because he has dealt bountifully with me.

(Psalm 13:5-6)

Opening Activity

Ask the group to form as wide a circle as possible. Invite participants to think of the center of the circle as God. Ask everyone to take three steps to move farther away from the center of the circle, and note how this changes the distance of each participant both from God and from each other. As participants return to their original positions, ask everyone to take three steps toward the center, and note how moving closer to God also affects the distance between people. Explain that this exercise is more than 1,500 years old. It was devised by a Christian monk in the Egyptian desert who wanted to show people the relationship between drawing closer to God and drawing closer to our fellow human beings; in other words, he wanted to show people the path to the good life.

LEARNING TOGETHER

Key Insights

1. The popular idea that pleasure, material wealth, and career success are the path to the good life is really a dead end.
2. For those who define success and security by material wealth, more is never enough. Our nation's experience over the past fifty years—which saw both a rising standard of living and a declining level of happiness—is evidence that money can't buy fulfillment in life.
3. We need to redefine what the good life means, turning away from measuring it only in terms of wealth or success and turning

toward the more holistic idea captured in the Greek word *eudaimonia*, which means "human flourishing."

4. Along with cultivating gratitude, pursuing a purpose bigger than ourselves, living beneath our means, and defining ourselves by generosity—all markers on the pathway that leads to true happiness—we find one of the keys to the good life when we invest in relationships with other people.
5. Beyond close relationships with family and friends, we experience the good life when we work toward the good of others, recognizing that God blesses us so that we might in turn be a blessing.
6. The entirety of Scripture teaches that the good life God wants for us is lived in relationship with others. Jesus summed up that teaching when he said that the greatest commandments were to love God and to love our neighbors. When we live by these commandments, we pass from death into life.
7. We find the good life of fulfillment when we trust in God.
8. Trusting in God does not mean we will experience material wealth or will not experience hardship or suffering. It means that we will experience peace and fulfillment that transcend everything else.
9. When we can experience the good life in the midst of adversity, we know our faith is real.

Leader Extra: Remaining Awake Through a Great Revolution

The last Sunday sermon by Dr. Martin Luther King, preached at Washington DC's National Cathedral, was titled "Remaining Awake Through a Great Revolution." In the sermon he recounted the story of the rich man and Lazarus the beggar (Luke 16:19-31). Why, King asked, did poor Lazarus wind up "in the bosom of Abraham" and the rich man (often called Dives) wind up separated from heaven by a vast chasm? It wasn't because of the rich man's wealth, King said. After all, Abraham was one of the richest people of his time. The rich man's real sin, King said, was that "he allowed his brother to become invisible," even though Lazarus sat outside the gate of Dives' mansion every day, hoping to eat the crumbs that the servants threw out. "Dives didn't realize that his wealth was his opportunity," King said. "It was his opportunity to bridge the gulf that separated him from his brother Lazarus." Similarly, preached King, America in 1968 faced an opportunity to use its great wealth to help bridge the gulf between those who had an abundance and those who were suffering. The question was whether we would have the will to act or would choose to let our neighbors remain invisible to us.

Group Discussion

1. If you were going to create a "Happiness Index," what measures would you use as elements that contribute to total happiness? How would you rank your community according to these measures? (You might also try creating a "Stress Index.")
2. Read Psalm 46. In times of trouble, how do you find refuge in God?
3. Where in your life do you find a purpose bigger than yourself? How does this purpose contribute to your sense of happiness and fulfillment?
4. In what ways do you believe your church has been blessed in order to be a blessing?
5. When have you found that our culture makes it difficult to redefine the good life in ways that do not involve wealth and material goods? Where have you found help and encouragement in standing against that culture?
6. The "prosperity gospel" that is popular among many Christians teaches that God wants us to be financially successful. Do you disagree with that? If so, what would you say to someone who preaches the prosperity gospel?

7. Read Matthew 7:24-27. Where in our society do you see houses built on sand? Where do you see houses built on solid rock?
8. Read Matthew 11:2-6. In this passage, how does Jesus define his ministry in terms of relationships with other people? How are acts of healing a sign of the presence of God's kingdom? Where can you work to provide healing? What do you think Jesus meant in saying he came to bring good news to the poor?
9. Read Matthew 6:25-34. What does it mean to trust completely in God for what we need? How difficult do you find it to follow Jesus' teaching not to worry about tomorrow? Do you think this level of radical trust is even possible?
10. When have you discovered freedom in the act of letting go of material things? When have you found freedom at times when you stopped worrying about personal success?
11. Reread the story of the fall of Adam and Eve in Genesis 3:1-12, bearing in mind that the Hebrew word for "naked" also translates as "vulnerable." How did Adam and Eve's perceived vulnerability change their relationship with God? How does a failure of trust affect our own relationship with God?
12. How has this discussion helped or challenged you?

Group Activity

Drawing on the Leader Extra: Remaining Awake Through a Great Revolution to provide background, read Luke 16:19-31 and then ask the group to reimagine Jesus' story from the rich man's point of view. Consider what the rich man might have felt upon seeing the beggar Lazarus outside his gate every day. Ask the group to imagine three different endings to this story had the rich man heard Martin Luther King's sermon and taken its message to heart. Discuss how these alternative scenarios might have enabled the rich man to find the good life. Discuss also how, beyond his material needs, an alternative ending might have offered more of the good life to the beggar in the here and now. How, beyond meeting Lazarus's material needs, would a change of heart by the rich man have provided the "good news to the poor" of which Jesus spoke?

WRAPPING UP

Taking It to Heart This Week

Briefly review the "Taking It to Heart This Week" exercises included in this week's Participant Handout. Encourage participants to complete the activities during the coming week.

Notable Quote

> *"John...describes the good life this way: "We know that we have passed from death to life because we love one another" (1 John 3:14). We see death in this life, but we move from death into the life that God intends for us when we love others, when we care for them, when we bless them, when we seek to serve, when we put the others' needs before our own. When we are doing those things, we live the life of love."*
>
> —*Adam Hamilton*

Closing Prayer

O God, we thank you for life. You walk with us every moment of every day. You stand with us when we go through hard times. You fill our hearts with peace and joy when otherwise we would be afraid. Everything we are and everything we have comes from you. Please help us to remember what really matters. Help us to be grateful for what we have. Help us to find your purpose for us and try to live it. Help us to take seriously our relationships with our family and friends and to invest in them, that we might be used by you to make this world a better place. Help us to trust in you and to love you with all that we are and all that we have. In Jesus' name. Amen.

WEEK 5:
LIVING THE GOOD LIFE
PARTICIPANT HANDOUT

We know that we have passed from death to life because we love one another.

(1 John 3:14)

Key Insights

1. The popular idea that pleasure, material wealth, and career success are the path to the good life is really a dead end.
2. For those who define success and security by material wealth, more is never enough. Our nation's experience over the past fifty years—which saw both a rising standard of living and a declining level of happiness—is evidence that money can't buy fulfillment in life.
3. We need to redefine what the good life means, turning away from measuring it only in terms of wealth or success and turning toward the more holistic idea captured in the Greek word *eudaimonia*, which means "human flourishing."
4. Along with cultivating gratitude, pursuing a purpose bigger than ourselves, living beneath our means, and defining ourselves by generosity—all markers on the pathway that leads to true happiness—we find one of the keys to the good life when we invest in relationships with other people.
5. Beyond close relationships with family and friends, we experience the good life when we work toward the good of others, recognizing that God blesses us so that we might in turn be a blessing.

6. The entirety of Scripture teaches that the good life God wants for us is lived in relationship with others. Jesus summed up that teaching when he said that the greatest commandments were to love God and to love our neighbors. When we live by these commandments, we pass from death into life.
7. We find the good life of fulfillment when we trust in God.
8. Trusting in God does not mean we will experience material wealth or will not experience hardship or suffering. It means that we will experience peace and fulfillment that transcend everything else.
9. When we can experience the good life in the midst of adversity, we know our faith is real.

Taking It to Heart This Week

- What things give you the most pleasure in your day-to-day life?
- What things cause you stress?
- How might you adjust your priorities to reduce your stress and gain a greater sense of fulfillment in life?
- How much would you need to let go and trust God in order to change your priorities? What might this consist of doing?